BRAGGING RIGHTS™

HIGH-IMPACT EMPLOYEE RECOGNITION

OTHER WIN-WINS@WORK PRODUCTS FROM FRANKLIN COVEY

Congrats Pack™
You Rock Cards™
Win-Wins@Work Magnet
Win-Wins@Work Bookmark
What Counts: How Forward Thinking Leaders Recognize and Reward Employees
Warriors@Work: What the Smartest Business Leaders Are Saying

Concept by Cheryl Kerzner
Design by Kim Louie and Dan Longhurst
Written by Debra Harris and Sunny Larson

Manufactured in United States of America

 FranklinCovey™

INTRODUCTION

To keep energized and excited about work, employees need to know their contributions make a difference. They need to be routinely rewarded for their performance. But to make it clear that you appreciate it when someone puts in a big effort, takes on new challenges, or successfully turns around a problem means having simple recognition tools at hand. With WIN-WINS@WORK, you never have to miss another opportunity to informally recognize an employee on the spot.

The WIN-WINS@WORK line was created with the belief that recognition doesn't have to be time-consuming or a big production. Celebrating accomplishments, acknowledging individuals and teams, recognizing outstanding efforts, and fostering a climate of encouragement are key to improving morale, productivity, and work quality. Our hope is that managers on all levels will use this book to brag a little or a lot about outstanding achievements. After all, a little praise goes a long way.

talent alert

YOUR IDEAS ARE OUTSTANDING

no fear

THANKS FOR YOUR BRAVE THINKING

great work

I'M IMPRESSED

thanks for staying late

I APPRECIATE YOUR DEDICATION

brilliant idea

YOU MAKE US LOOK GOOD

bravo

THANKS FOR STAYING ON TOP OF THINGS

kicked
upstairs

CONGRATS ON THE PROMOTION

great meeting

YOUR ENTHUSIASM IS CONTAGIOUS

job well done
YOU HANDLED IT LIKE A PRO

you're an asset to our team

THANKS FOR THE EXCELLENT WORK

big thanks

FOR YOUR BIG IDEAS

you rock

THANKS FOR YOUR HARD WORK

where would we be without you?

THANKS FOR THE EXCELLENT WORK

i hear you

THANKS FOR THE FEEDBACK

thanks

FOR GETTING IT ALL DONE ON TIME

talent alert

YOUR IDEAS ARE OUTSTANDING

no fear

THANKS FOR YOUR BRAVE THINKING

great work

I'M IMPRESSED

thanks for staying late

I APPRECIATE YOUR DEDICATION

brilliant idea

YOU MAKE US LOOK GOOD

bravo

THANKS FOR STAYING ON TOP OF THINGS

kicked
upstairs

CONGRATS ON THE PROMOTION

great
meeting

YOUR ENTHUSIASM IS CONTAGIOUS

job well done
YOU HANDLED IT LIKE A PRO

you're an asset to our team

THANKS FOR THE EXCELLENT WORK

big thanks

FOR YOUR BIG IDEAS

you rock

THANKS FOR YOUR HARD WORK

where would we be without you?

THANKS FOR THE EXCELLENT WORK

i hear you

THANKS FOR THE FEEDBACK